180 Degrees

in

180 Days

KORY NELSON

Fulton Books
Meadville, PA

Published by Fulton Books 2024

ISBN 979-8-88982-669-9 (paperback)
ISBN 979-8-88982-670-5 (digital)

Printed in the United States of America

Once it seemed like only a myth, a dream, an urban legend if you will. I had tried to complete this task once before, only to fall flat on my face after forty-seven days and only turning my direction in life by 50 degrees or so, coming nowhere even close to my desired destination of 180 degrees and nowhere even close to my goal of 180 days of sobriety. Now some might wonder why the 180-degree mark is so important. It's important because, for the last few years I have just been going in circles, and if I were to go 360 degrees and go full circle now; then I would end up exactly where

I am today, which may sound great because I am doing well and I am proud of myself. But if I went in a circle, that would mean I would go up in life, but then I would also have a big letdown to go with that up. Instead, I want to do 180 degrees; that way when I reach the top of that circle, I can break the cycle there and stay clean and just keep going up in life and put and leave addiction and drugs in my past and in my old circle. I do that by attending these meetings and surrounding myself with good positive people, and not putting myself in bad situations or bad areas where I know that I shouldn't be. Now after failing on this quest once before I knew that I had a daunting task ahead of me and one that seemed most definitely improbable, if not impossible. Now here I am on day 180. I seemed to have made it to my 180-day goal time-wise anyway. Now what about my directional goal of turning my life around 180 degrees?

I went from only seeing my family maybe five times in six years and missing the last three Thanksgivings and three Christmases to spending every one of these 180 days living and being around family, and you best believe I did not miss Thanksgiving or Christmas this year. Spending Thanksgiving in Pahrump, Nevada, at my grandparent's house, whom I also hadn't seen in over six years. Then for Christmas, we went back to New Mexico and spent the holidays at my brother's house with my parents, my sister, my brother and his wife, and my four amazing nephews that I missed the hell out of.

I went from wandering around like a zombie, cold and shivering on the streets and trying to figure out where I'm going to sleep for the night and worrying and wondering, *Will I be safe if I close my eyes, or is someone gonna try and rob me and take all of my shit or worse lay hands on me and try to touch me or hurt me?* Oftentimes too paranoid and honestly too damn scared to lie down somewhere and close my eyes and actually be able to get some much-needed rest. I went from that to having a warm, cozy house that I can set the temperature in it to however the hell I want it. With a comfy bed and comfy pillows, and as far as feeling safe is concerned, the house is alarmed with a security system, and the alarm is set every night before we go to bed.

I went from often starving and always being worried and thinking of how I was gonna eat and where my next meal was going to come from because I rarely ever actually had money, and if I did, you best believe that every single penny of that went to drugs because if it came down to food or drugs, the drugs won every time because I knew and I was afraid that I would get dope sick and my body would start going into an agonizing withdrawal. I also went from going into a store with every intention of stealing my food because I had no money to pay for it. Especially the good, expensive food, I made sure I got that because in my drugged-out state of mind my mindset was *Well, if I'm going to break the law, mine as well go big, go home, or go to jail. I'm homeless, so I ain't got no home. I sure as hell don't want to go back to jail. So if I'm gonna go take shit, I'm gonna go big.* I went from that to where I'm now, and now when I go into a store, I'm not all strung out and actually pay for my groceries like a normal person. I used to make sure that I got the biggest and best stuff out of the door without paying for it, and now I make sure that I don't leave the store without paying for even the smallest item like I did the other day when I was leaving the grocery store and I checked out and walked out to the car and realized I had a ninety-nine-cent pack of gum in my hand you know like the little five-pack Juicy Fruit gums that they have that say there only twenty-five cents, but they're really basically a dollar. So anyway, I was standing there and now realizing that I had accidentally taken this gum without paying for it. Without hesitation, I turned around and went back into the store and walked up to the cashier and said, "Oh, I'm sorry, I had this pack of gum in my hand, and I accidentally forgot to pay for it."

So the cashier said, "Oh okay, that's no problem. Thank you for your honesty. You wouldn't believe how many people would have just kept on going or wouldn't have planned on paying for it at all in the first place."

I smirked at her and said, "Oh yes, I would, because I used to be one of those people, and I'm trying to do good now and stay out of trouble."

So she said, "Well, good for you, but as far as you getting in trouble for this, I think you would have been okay because nobody saw you and nobody would have known," and I said, "No, that is not true."

She looked at me with a rather strange and weird look.

I said, "That's not true because I would still have known, and that's not okay with me."

She then asked me if I knew what the word *integrity* meant, and I said, "Well, yes, I do actually."

She said, "Well then, tell me what you think it is."

I said, "To me, *integrity* means to do the right thing even when nobody is watching," and she smiled at me and said, "Exactly. You may have made mistakes in your past, but that doesn't define who you are as a person unless you let it."

That really stuck with me when she said that. It wasn't about how much it costs, it was the principle of it.

Another thing that really stuck with me lately is when my mom and I were watching TV the other day and that commercial came on—you know, that one that sings that little song, "Walk a mile in my shoes, walk a mile in my shoes." Anyway, I looked over at my mom, and I said, "Hey, Mom, let's switch shoes, and I'll walk a mile in your shoes, and then you can walk a mile in my shoes."

Then she looked at me real seriously and real compassionately and sat there quiet for about thirty seconds and said, "You know what, Kory? Everything you have gone through and everything you have been through, I don't think I would have made it a mile in your shoes," and it brought a tear to my eyes, because I think she finally realized just how close she was to losing her baby forever and just how much pain and trauma I really went through. Because just a few weeks before that I broke down and cried when I read old messages that I had on my Facebook from my dad, never missing a birthday or a holiday and always saying he loved me no matter what. It was then after reading all of those messages from my dad that I realized just what I put them through, and now I saw the pain and world through their eyes and in her shoes, and now in that moment, I felt she saw the pain and trauma through my eyes and in my shoes.

I heard something on *Live PD* the other day that really had an impact on me. The scene was this: A young black man in his midtwenties was sitting there on a bridge with his feet dangling off the edge, and a cop pulls up. The cop waves at him to get his attention and to let him know that he was there so he didn't startle the guy. When the guy looked at the cop, he had tears in his eyes, and you could just see the pain on his face.

The guy looked away just for a second, and the cop reached around and bear-hugged the guy and pulled him off the ledge. Then the cop looked at him and grabbed his hand to hold and comfort the guy, and he told him, "Hey, big man, I can tell you're obviously going through a lot, and believe me I have been through a lot myself. I did two tours in Iraq and Kuwait and have been through a lot of mental health issues because of it." But he tells him that killing himself is not worth it, and never is. He tells him that suicide is a permanent solution to a temporary problem. I thought to myself and told my dad, "Wow, that is so true and on such a deep level." Then as I was writing this, I thought to myself, *Wow! Drugs are so similar to that yet so different at the same time because doing drugs is a temporary solution, but it is also the cause of a permanent problem.*

So now I feel we have covered the 180 degrees part. Now just to clarify the question of how long 180 days really is, well, 180 days was the ultimate goal but not always the immediate goal because like I said before, 180 days seemed impossible at times, especially in the beginning. There was a time when I would have laughed at the thought of me actually making it to 180 days, and now I laugh that I ever doubted myself in the first place. At times I had to make shorter and easier goals, like maybe 180 seconds at a time. After that, then I would aim for 180 minutes; and if I could achieve that, then I would try for a much harder goal of 180 hours because let's face it, 180 seconds is really only 3 minutes, and 180 minutes is only 3 hours. So how long is 180 hours? Well, that's when I found something very interesting: 180 hours actually breaks down to exactly 7.5 days, which is a crazy analogy if you think about it. To reach 180 hours in your goal, that would be 7.5 days. For most normal people, if you will, after 7 days their week is essentially over, and then they start a new one. But not addicts. We have to work that much harder than everyone else just to get back to feeling normal. Between our meetings and doctor's appointments and regulating and taking our meds, it takes us probably at least 12 hours or half a day, if you will, just for us to balance everything out in our life and our recovery every week; and that's just something we need to embrace instead of being discouraged about.

I was always taught that it's not about how hard you can hit in life but rather how hard you can get hit and get back up and keep fighting, and I'm fighting. I'm fighting for my health, I'm fighting for my sobriety, I'm fighting for my recovery, and I'm fighting for my sanity. I'm fighting for my pride and dignity, hoping that one day soon I will walk with my head held high because God knows these last few years I walked with my head down only looking up to see where I was going, not because there was something awesome or amazing on the ground but, because I had no pride and no self-respect, not even low self-esteem but no self-esteem—so much so that I would try to avoid windows or mirrors altogether because I did not want to see myself because for the first time in my life, when I saw my reflection, I didn't recognize the person that was staring back at me. But most importantly, I'm fighting for my life because I learned two things while on this journey that I will always hold onto and never forget: Life is beautiful, and life is precious, and I have lost more friends to this evil addiction than I can count. I'm fighting to tell my story. I'm fighting for me, I'm fighting for you, and I'm fighting for every one of us in this real life-or-death battle with addiction. We must unite and stick together and support and encourage each other. It's the only way we actually have a chance. I say this loud and I say this proud: I never gave up. No matter how bad things got, I never quit fighting, and I will never quit! I'll never quit on me, and I'll never quit on you. You can't quit on you because if we quit, then we will die. I think most addicts want to get clean, but they get nervous and are frightened by the thought of going through that withdrawal because honestly, it is brutal. However, recovery on the other side of it is so worth it. You can actually start living your life and be the real you again. If you are struggling with addiction, I highly recommend reaching out to someone and being open and honest about your struggle. We cannot do this on our own, and we do not have to do it alone. The opposite of addiction is connection.

On the streets in Phoenix, they have a term that they use when they see a cop. They say "one time," and when I asked somebody why do they say "one time" and what does it mean, they told me that they say "one time" when they see a cop to give everyone a heads-up that a cop is there and to be on your toes because it only takes that one time and your ass is going to jail. I was thinking about this recently and decided that my new nickname for all these opioids out there that everyone is hooked on is "One Time" because you never know what's in it, and if the chemicals are portioned correctly or not, and all it takes is that one hit or that "one time," and that's all she wrote. It truly is like playing a game of Russian Roulette with very real and deadly consequences; and that, my friends, is absolutely terrifying. It's like Colicchie says, "It's not just an epidemic, it's more like an apocalypse."

I went from being arrested on a warrant by the police, only to pass out and faint, falling face-first into concrete while going through the booking process and waking up several hours later in a hospital with a black eye, a busted-up nose, and a fat lip so swollen that I could barely fit a straw into my mouth to drink from. Now why did I faint and end up in the hospital, you might wonder? Well, you see, when I got to the hospital that night, they had to check all my vitals and run tests because I was unconscious and unresponsive for over four hours; and while running these tests, they discovered that I only weighed 110 pounds and they had to pump five pints of blood into my body. Yes, I said five pints of blood, which is absolutely crazy to think about because the average adult body normally has between about eight to ten pints of blood in it. So I had lost more than half of my blood from internal bleeding and had been basically slowly dying and bleeding out. Now you may ask yourself, how could I not have known that I was losing so much blood over this period of time? My answer to you is this: While at the peak of my addiction and my time on the streets, both in Albuquerque and in Phoenix, I neglected my health and literally treated my body like a human trash can while putting so many harmful chemicals into my system for so much time. Now how much time exactly? I put it to you like this: In the beginning, it was just to pass the hours—you know, something to do, and then that became days, and the days turned into weeks, and then the weeks transitioned into months; and before I knew it, those months had become years. It was like an amazing dream that you never wanted to end, but then you slowly realized that you are in a never-ending dream and that you will never be able to leave and you are now a slave to this dream, and then boom! Something happens that allows you to wake up and realize that this really never was a happy dream. But instead, you realize that you had been mistaken, deceived, lied to, and manipulated by this so-called dream that you now can finally see it for what it really is, and that dream, in actual reality, is no dream at all but rather it is a *nightmare*! I went from that to where I'm now. I now walk around at 145 pounds; and even though my health will never be perfect, let alone great, comparing the two would be like comparing a nightmare to a dream. Finally, I went from being a lost and confused man with what felt like no purpose and not much will to live, to a man that I can honestly say for the first time in what feels like forever, is actually filled with hope and belief that great things are to come and are just on the horizon. To anyone out there that reads this that is going through a hard time, I just want to say to you that I know things may seem difficult in life at the moment, but I promise you there are sunnier days to come after all of these clouds and rain and that things and life will eventually get better because this, too, shall pass!

This is in 2010 on a cruise for my sister's graduation. This is me, my mom, my dad, and my sister. I was clean at the time here. Life used to be so much easier back then.

That's my older brother, sister, and myself in 2014.
I was clean and doing good here. I'm the baby
and runt of the litter. They both like to call me
"midget" even though I'm taller than my sister

This is in 2015 when I became an assistant store director and had 165 people working for me. I was in Salt Lake City here for manager training for fifteen weeks. I was doing good in life here, except I had a drinking problem that nobody knew about. I didn't want people to think of me negatively given my prior struggles with addiction, so I just kept my struggle to myself. On the surface, everything looked good, but looks can be deceiving.

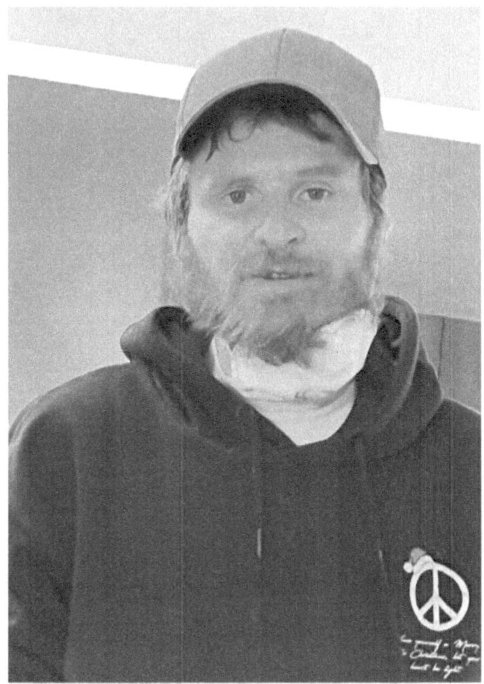

This is me after being homeless on the streets for two years. This is day one of this current journey that I'm on. We should try not to judge other people because we never know what someone may be going through or dealing with. I used to get prescribed pills, and then I started abusing them and self medicating, and I started buying pills off the streets and then that led to me ending up on the streets. It is a vicious cycle, and it is way to common in the world we live in today.

Day one: Addiction is not funny, it is not a game, and this is what could happen if we do not take our problems seriously. Whenever we feel like complaining about the problems in our own lives, we really should just try to remind ourselves to be grateful because I promise you that someone out there always has it worse than we do. Even when I was homeless, there was always someone out there that I met that had it worse than I did.

This photo is from Thanksgiving 2022 at my grandparent's house in Pahrump, Nevada. I'm ninety days clean here. This journey that I have gone on has really put life in perspective for me and showed me what really matters and what's actually important, and to me, that is family. I'm so thankful for this time that I have gotten to spend with my family, especially my grandparents on my mom's side.

This is from my graduation from the Community Court Program in Mesa, Arizona. I actually read *180 Degrees in 180 Days* to the judge and all the cops and prosecutors that day. I got a standing ovation and was asked for a copy of it. Someday I hope that my story is in drug court programs all over the country because I think that my story could possibly make a difference. Knowledge is power, and the more information and resources out there, the better. Even if my story could help just one person not have to go through everything that I went through, I would be happy. This is day 180.

This is May 2023. This is my oldest nephew; he just graduated high school, and this was Senior Day. I'm so happy that I got sober and was actually able to see him play one last time! He is such a talented musician, and he is so kind yet so strong at the same time. You can do anything that you set your mind to nephew. I believe in you. The world is yours for the taking, you just have to take it. You have come so far in life. To say that I'm a proud uncle, well, that would be an understatement. You will do great things, and the best is yet to come. I love you, bud!

This is from Memorial Day 2023. I had just gotten flowers with my parents to go visit my grandpa's grave. He was a veteran who fought in the Navy, in the Korean War. He is buried at the National Veterans Cemetery in Santa Fe, New Mexico. I got in some trouble growing up, so he used to call me "Al," short for Al Capone, as a joke.

This is in celebration of my one year in recovery! This is my beautiful momma and my amazing dad. I would not be here today if it weren't for them. They never turned their back on me and never gave up on me. I cannot thank them enough for the support and love they have given me. They are my rock and truly are the best parents that a guy could ask for. I love you both very much. Thank you for always being there for me!

This is my grandparents on my mom's side. We were
celebrating my grandpa's birthday. I am 1 year clean
in this picture. They are very kind people, and they
are both very religious as well. My renewed faith
in God has opened up an opportunity for great
conversations with my grandma, we have had multiple,
several hours—long conversations because of it.

Tonight I went to the church and received my 1 year in recovery chip! As soon as I admitted that I had a problem, and opened up about my addiction, my life has never been the same since. If anyone out there is struggling, please just hang in there, because eventually things will get better. Do not let other people tell you that you are not enough, and that it's impossible for you to get clean and get your life back. I'm living proof that it is possible. Impossible is an opinion, not a fact.

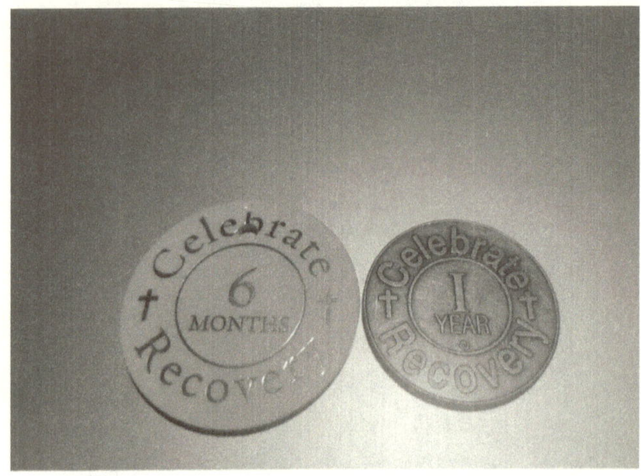

There were times that I didn't think that 6 months was possible; let alone a year. I'm proud of myself for making it this far, one down, many more to come! I truly do believe that my life being spared was an act of God! I would not be where I am today if it were not for my faith in God. All glory to God!

This is my Grammy, and my brother, and I. This is 2016 shortly before I relapsed. My relationship of 2 years ended the same week that I lost my job, and I went into a crazy bad depression and was the start of the hell I went through for the next 6 Years. My Grammy and I were extremely close. I was her Kor Kor, and man did she love me, and man did I love her. We lived together for years, and she was always there for me. Even if she would be mad or disappointed in me, and believe me that happened alot. It still never changed the unconditional love that she had for me. I was 47 days clean and she died and I took it extremely hard. I relapsed again for about 5 months, and then I finally had enough and decided after almost dying, that this was it and I had to get my life together, or I was gonna die. I decided I want to try and make my Grammy proud. May she rest in peace.

I got this tattoo in honor of my Grammy. Her name
was Lucille Carol Nelson-Sanders but everyone called
her Lucy. She was one of the most amazing people
I have ever met, she taught me morals and respect,
and what it meant to be a gentleman, and taught me
that chivalry is not dead. She would get mad if I had
dirt under my fingernails. If I ever tried lying to her,
she would tell me that, "I need to stop fibbing". A lie
to her was a fib, and she was the only person I ever
heard say this. She also would tell me something that
I'll never forget. She would tell me that, "If you treat
me good, I'll treat you better". If I ever talked back to
her, she would call me a "little twerp". My 180 days
clean is actually on her birthday, I feel like she died
so that I could live. Through death, comes life.
I miss you very much and I hope your proud
of me. I would like to dedicate this book
to her. This one is for you Gram!

About the Author

Kory Wade Nelson is a thirty-three-year-old author from Albuquerque, New Mexico. He was born in Idaho Falls, Idaho. He recently moved to Phoenix, Arizona, for a fresh start. He broke his wrist when he was fifteen years old and was prescribed opioid painkillers. He has struggled with addiction to both narcotics and alcohol on and off ever since. This disease has had devastating impacts on his life. He went from being a successful retail manager with 165 people that worked for him, with his own apartment and car, to ending up homeless for over two years. Never in a million years would he have guessed he would end up homeless, but then COVID-19 happened. He lost his job, and everything closed down. He ended up living on the streets for almost all of the pandemic. While on the streets, his life began to spiral even more out of control. He found himself walking through the doors of our criminal justice system. Once you step foot through that front door, that front door turns into a revolving door. His substance abuse problem only got worse. He began struggling with other mental health issues like anxiety and depression. He is currently eighteen months clean!